PLANT CELLS
VS. ANIMAL CELLS

SIMILARITIES AND DIFFERENCES

Cells for Kids | Science Book for Grade 5
Children's Biology Books

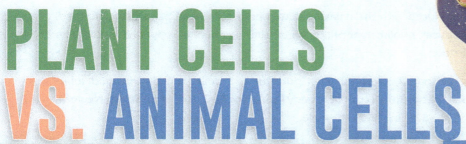

BABY PROFESSOR
EDUCATION KIDS

First Edition, 2021

Published in the United States by Speedy Publishing LLC, 40 E Main Street, Newark, Delaware 19711 USA.

© 2021 Baby Professor Books, an imprint of Speedy Publishing LLC

Baby Professor Books are available at special discounts when purchased in bulk for industrial and sales-promotional use. For details contact our Special Sales Team at Speedy Publishing LLC, 40 E Main Street, Newark, Delaware 19711 USA. Telephone (888) 248-4521 Fax: (210) 519-4043.

10 9 8 7 6 * 5 4 3 2 1

Print Edition: 9781541981171
Digital Edition: 9781541981300
Hardcover Edition: 9781541986886

See the world in pictures. Build your knowledge in style.
www.speedypublishing.com

TABLE OF CONTENTS

Young boy and a toddler together in a zoo watching giraffes and other animals.

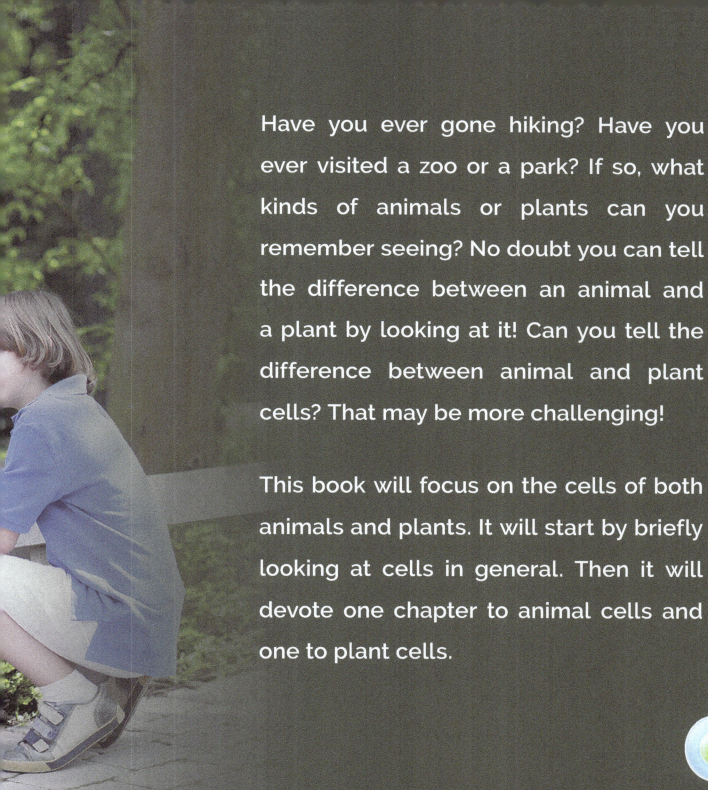

Have you ever gone hiking? Have you ever visited a zoo or a park? If so, what kinds of animals or plants can you remember seeing? No doubt you can tell the difference between an animal and a plant by looking at it! Can you tell the difference between animal and plant cells? That may be more challenging!

This book will focus on the cells of both animals and plants. It will start by briefly looking at cells in general. Then it will devote one chapter to animal cells and one to plant cells.

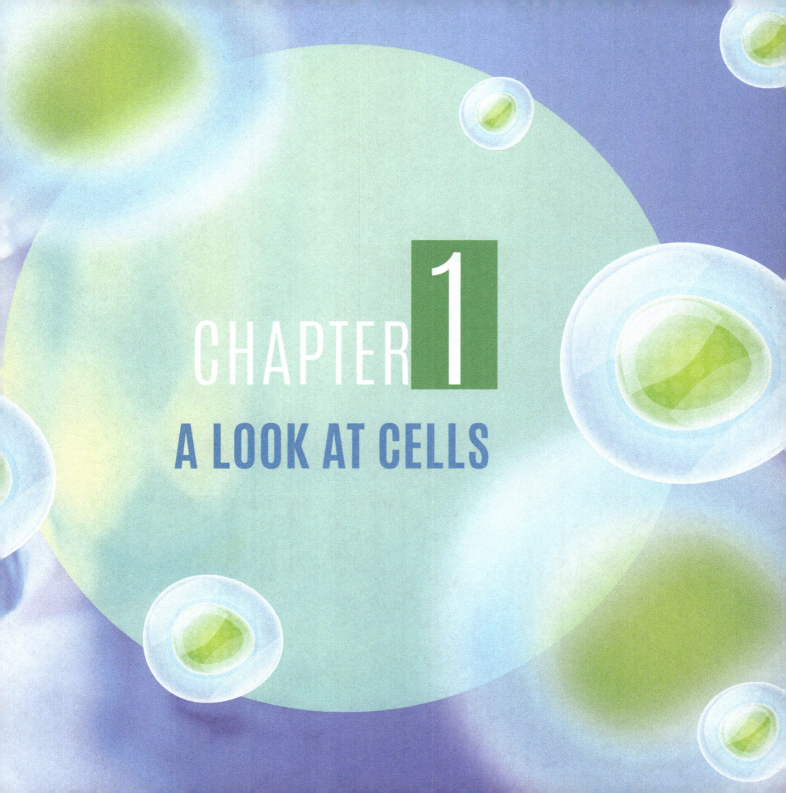

CHAPTER 1

A LOOK AT CELLS

Anything that is alive is comprised of cells. That includes both plants and animals. Comprised means contains or is made up of. Biology means the study of living things. A focus on studying cells is one branch of Biology.

Both plants and animals are made up of cells.

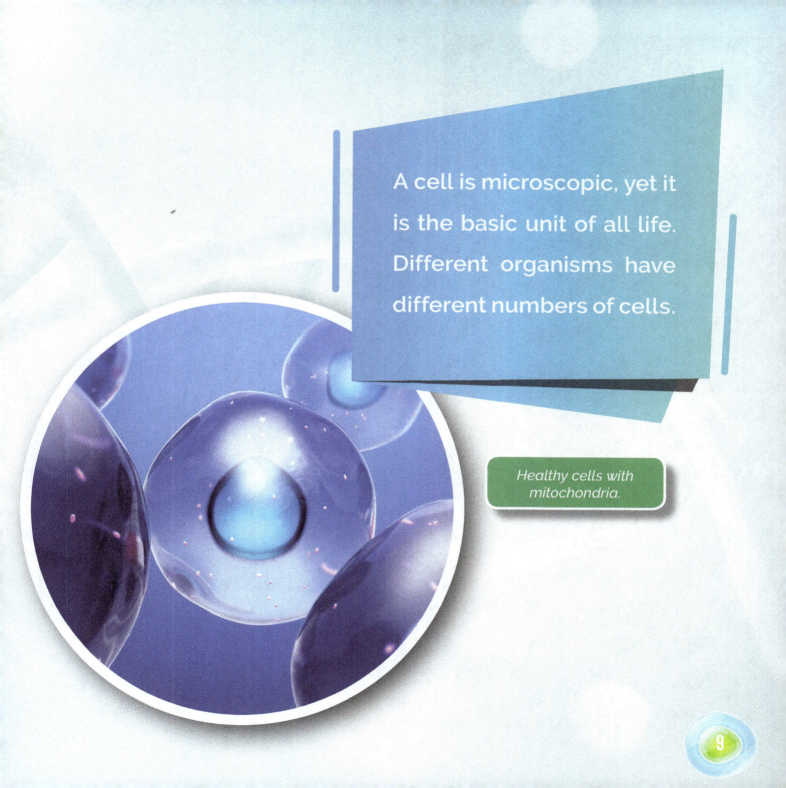

A cell is microscopic, yet it is the basic unit of all life. Different organisms have different numbers of cells.

Healthy cells with mitochondria.

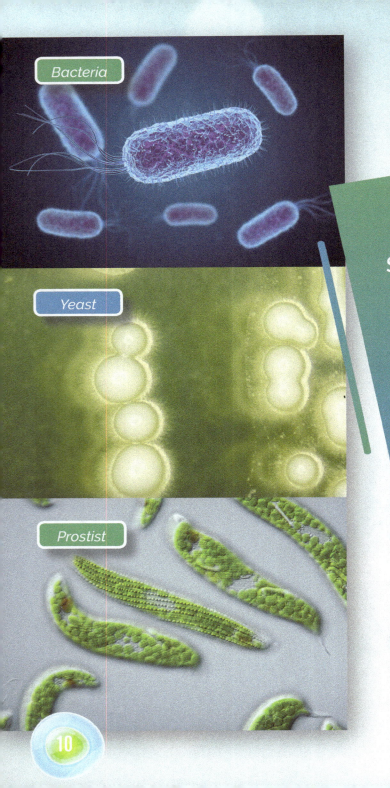

Bacteria

Yeast

Prostist

Some organisms only have one cell. They are unicellular organisms. Examples include bacteria, yeast, and protists. Everything that is necessary to maintain life is done in that one cell!

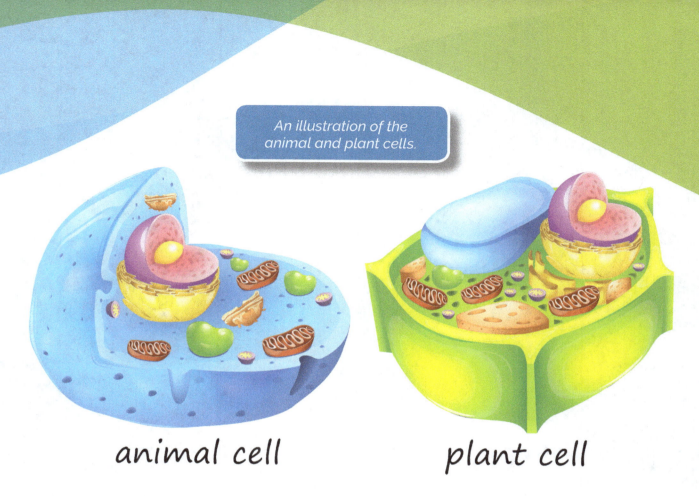

An illustration of the animal and plant cells.

animal cell   plant cell

Other organisms that are big are comprised of billions of them! They are multicellular organisms. The two most common multicellular organisms are animals and plants. One person has more than 75 trillion cells!

Antonie van Leeuwenhoek

12

DID YOU KNOW?

A Dutch scientist named Anton van Leeuwenhoek was one of the first people to research unicellular organisms, also called single-celled organisms. When he viewed them, they reminded him of small animals. For this reason, he started to call them animalcules. This interesting name prompted other scientists to study them as well.

Microscope discoveries by Antonie van Leeuwenhoek

13

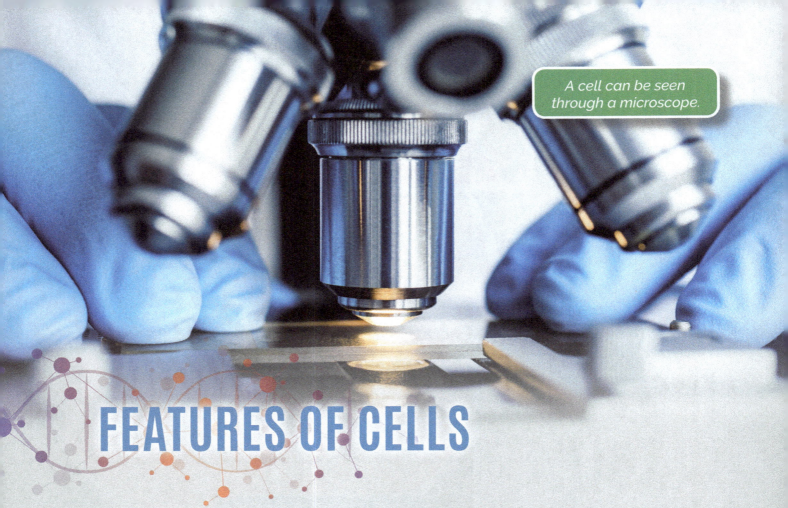

A cell can be seen through a microscope.

FEATURES OF CELLS

A cell can be big or small. Remember that you still need a microscope to view it. A cell can also come in different shapes. Despite the size or shape of a cell, all cells carry out certain functions.

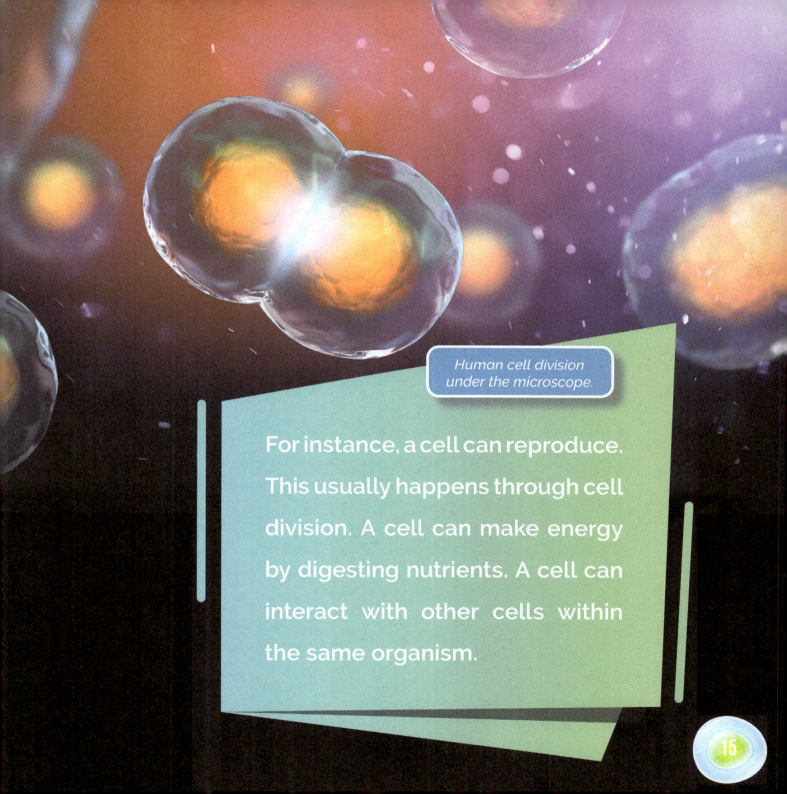

For instance, a cell can reproduce. This usually happens through cell division. A cell can make energy by digesting nutrients. A cell can interact with other cells within the same organism.

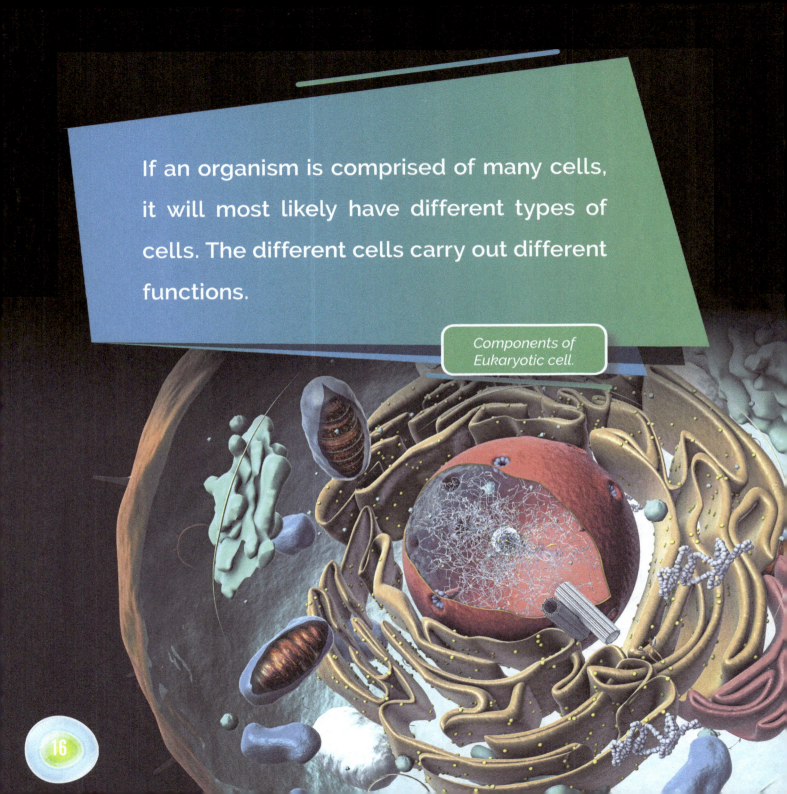

If an organism is comprised of many cells, it will most likely have different types of cells. The different cells carry out different functions.

Components of Eukaryotic cell.

Zebra showing its teeth

Orange tree with flowers and fruit.

For instance, an animal will have certain cells that will only make teeth or muscle. A plant will have certain cells that function to make seeds, fruit, or flowers.

MAIN PARTS OF CELLS

Almost every cell consists of three distinct parts. One is the cell membrane. This functions as the skin of the cell. The second is the cytoplasm. This part is responsible for doing different things to maintain the life of the cell. The third is the nucleus. This part functions as the brain of the cell. Nonetheless, some cells, like bacteria, do not have a nucleus. They only have a cell membrane and cytoplasm.

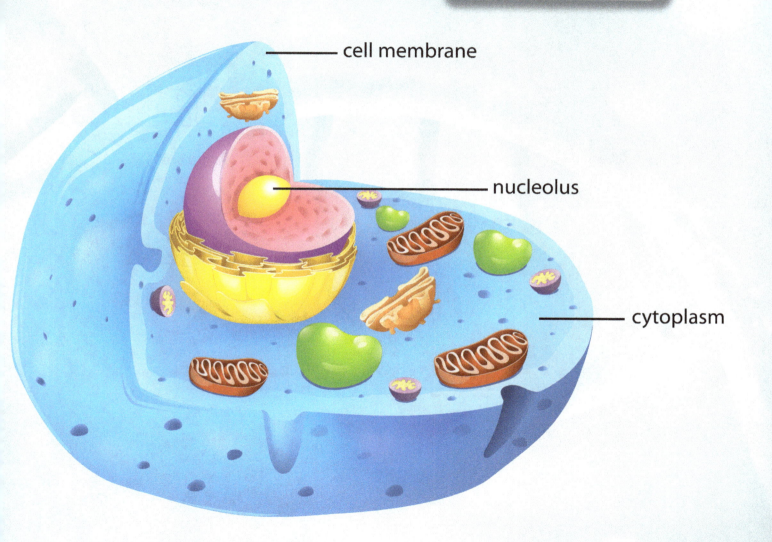

Three distinct parts of a cell.

cell membrane

nucleolus

cytoplasm

Cells differ depending on the type of organism in which they are found. This happens even though all cells have some things in common.

Structures of plant, animal and fungus cells.

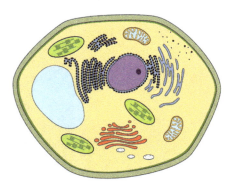

Plant cell

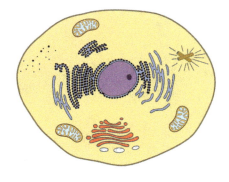

Animal cell

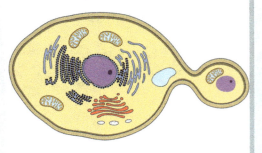

Fungus cell

DID YOU KNOW?

The simplest kind of cells are known as prokaryotic cells. An organism with this type of cell is a unicellular organism. The DNA in this type of cell moves about while clumped together. This type of cell has no organelles to carry out special jobs or help the cell to function.

PROKARYOTIC CELL

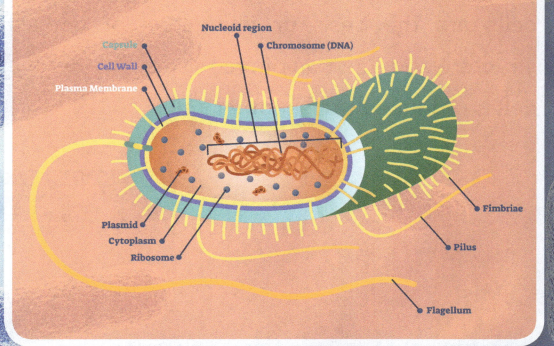

Nucleoid region

Capsule

Chromosome (DNA)

Cell Wall

Plasma Membrane

Plasmid

Cytoplasm

Ribosome

Fimbriae

Pilus

Flagellum

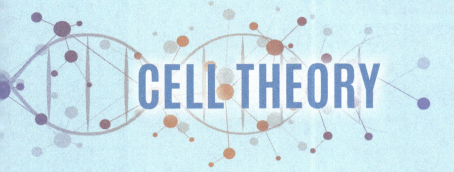

CELL THEORY

Cell theory refers to three characteristics of cells. Firstly, cells make up every organism. Secondly, cells are the basis or foundation of both the structure and function of organisms. Thirdly, every cell is produced from another cell.

All living organisms are made up of cells.

22

ANIMALS AND PLANTS

Animals receive energy by eating food. For this reason, they are known as consumers.

A monkey eating a banana.

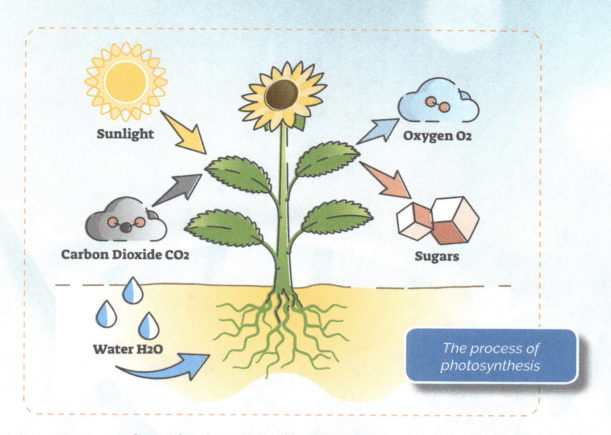

Sunlight

Carbon Dioxide CO₂

Water H₂O

Oxygen O₂

Sugars

The process of photosynthesis

Plants can make their own food. It happens through a process called photosynthesis. For this reason, plants are known as producers. In addition to making their own food, they are a source of food for animals.

Because animals and plants have different functions, their cells are not all the same.

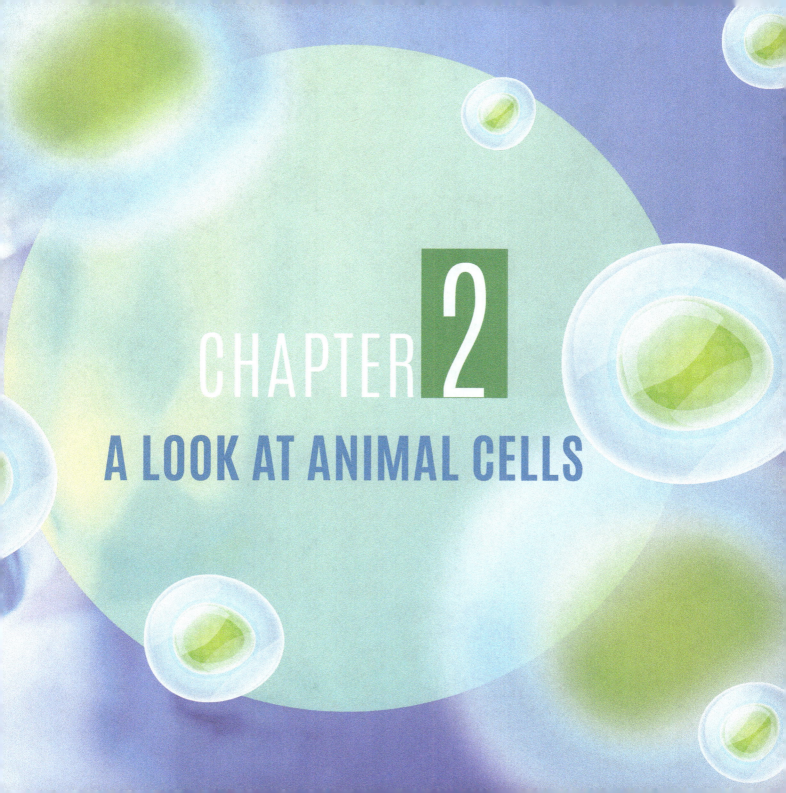

CHAPTER 2

A LOOK AT ANIMAL CELLS

The cells of different animals bear a resemblance to each other. They contain different parts.

A collage of different animals.

THE CELL MEMBRANE AND CYTOPLASM

They have a cell membrane which protects the cell. This membrane forms a barrier so that the cell is separated from anything outside its borders. Inside it is cytoplasm. This is a fluid that is gooey or jelly-like.

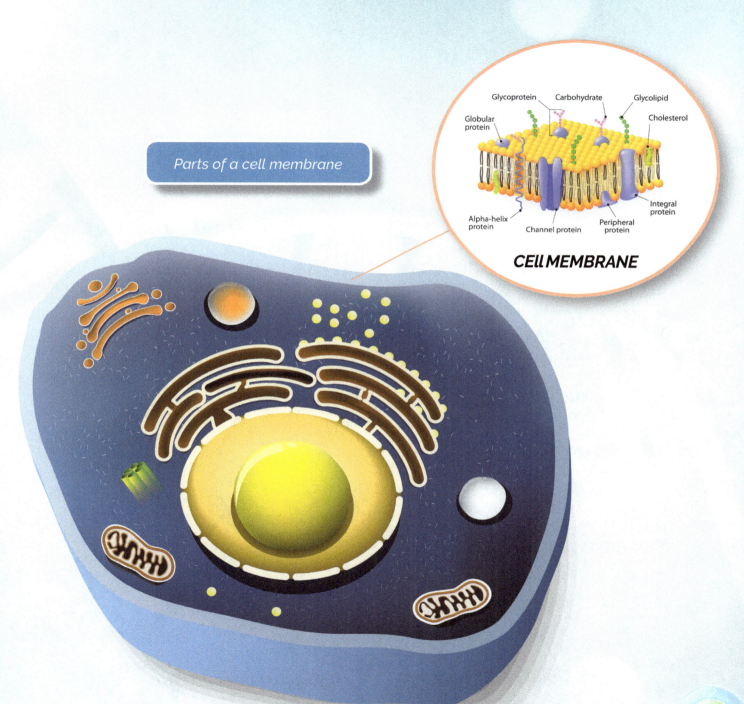

Parts of a cell membrane

Glycoprotein   Carbohydrate   Glycolipid

Globular
protein   Cholesterol

Alpha-helix
protein   Channel protein   Peripheral
protein   Integral
protein

CELL MEMBRANE

ORGANELLES

There are different organelles that float inside the cytoplasm. They take care of all the cell's needs.

Cell organelles

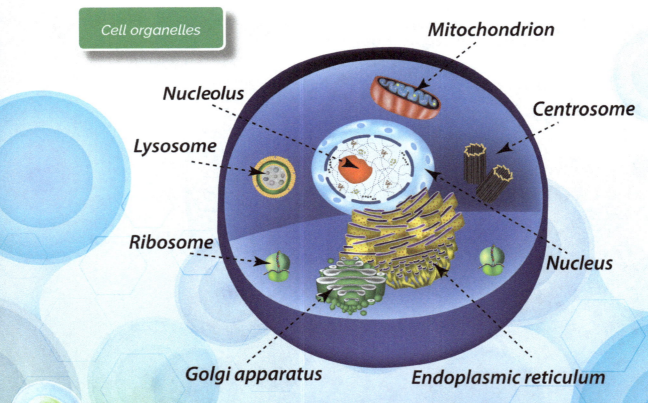

Mitochondrion

Nucleolus

Centrosome

Lysosome

Ribosome

Nucleus

Golgi apparatus

Endoplasmic reticulum

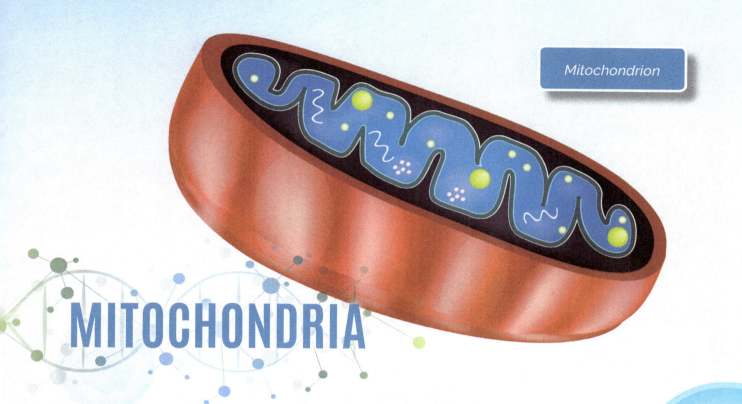

MITOCHONDRIA

A mitochondrion is an example of an organelle. It is shaped like an oval. Mitochondrion is the singular of mitochondria. There are many of them in the cytoplasm. They supply the cell with energy. Even though they are inside the cell membrane, they have a double membrane of their own!

The membrane on the inside has many folds. These are called cristae. There are electron transport chains there. These chains make ATP from sugar. ATP stands for adenosine triphosphate. They hold a lot of chemical energy. When ATP breaks down, energy is released. This is an important part of respiration. Respiration is how we gain energy; a part of the process is breathing!

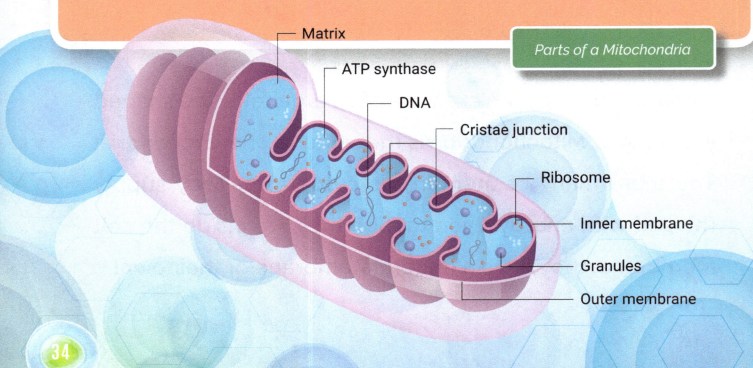

Parts of a Mitochondria

Matrix

ATP synthase

DNA

Cristae junction

Ribosome

Inner membrane

Granules

Outer membrane

THE NUCLEUS

Another organelle is the nucleus. It controls cell functions. It comes with its own membrane. Chromosomes are found in the nucleus. They are extremely tiny structures that carry DNA.

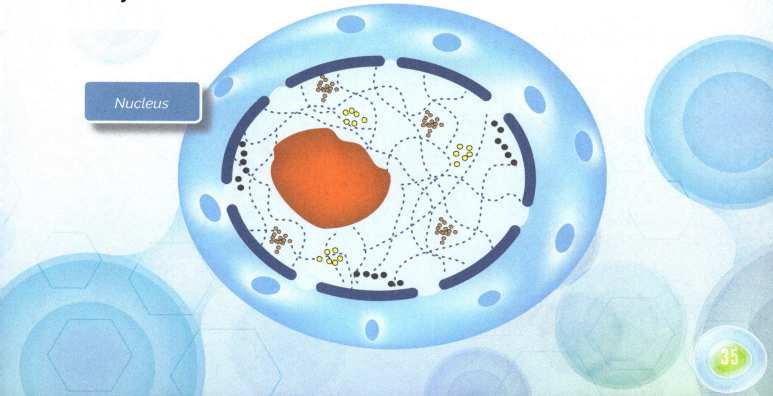

Nucleus

DNA stands for deoxyribonucleic acid. It contains all the hereditary material for the organism. Hereditary refers to the traits that an organism will inherit from its parents. In other words, the DNA is the blueprint for building an organism's body. Genes are made up of this material. RNA, which stands for ribonucleic acid, is also found in chromosomes. Different proteins are there as well.

An illustration of the differences in the structure of the DNA and RNA molecules.

DIFFERENCES BETWEEN DNA & RNA

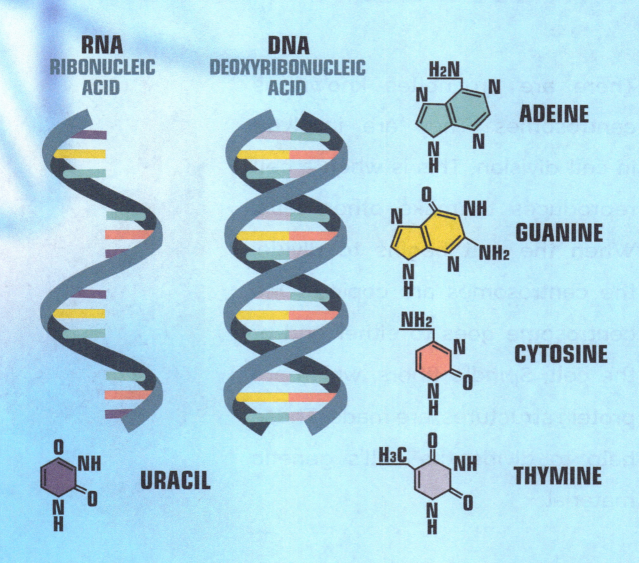

RNA
RIBONUCLEIC ACID

DNA
DEOXYRIBONUCLEIC ACID

ADEINE

GUANINE

CYTOSINE

URACIL

THYMINE

CENTROSOMES

There are organelles known as centrosomes. They are involved in cell division. This is when a cell reproduces to make other cells. When the cell begins to divide, the centrosomes are copied. One centrosome goes to either end of the cell. Spindle fibers, which are protein structures, are made. These help to divide the cell's genetic material.

Centrosomes

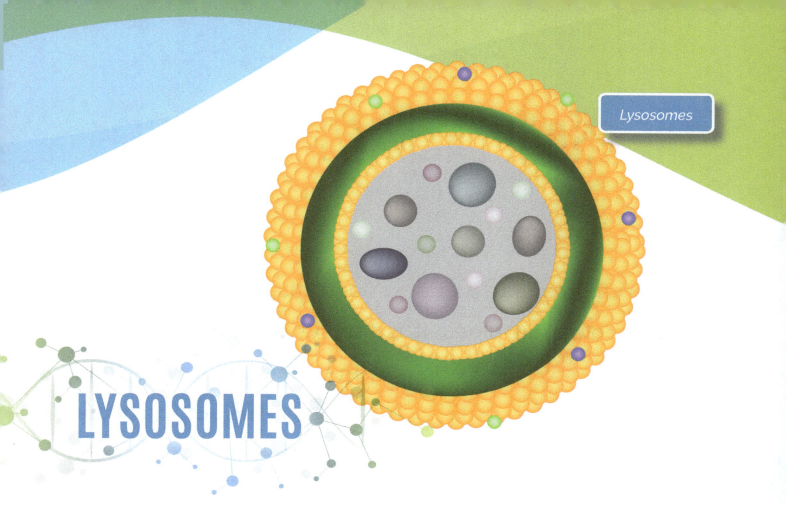

Lysosomes

LYSOSOMES

There are organelles known as lysosomes. They digest the nutrients for the cell. They have digestive enzymes which aid in the process. These enzymes can destroy the cell when they are released into it.

THE ENDOPLASMIC RETICULUM

This is an organelle that also floats inside the cytoplasm. It resembles flat pipes. It is the system by which other materials can travel within the cell. The outside of the endoplasmic reticulum can be smooth or rough. When it is rough it has ribosomes attached to it.

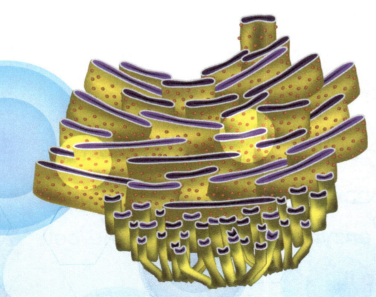

Endoplasmic Reticulum

RIBOSOMES

These are organelles that are responsible for producing protein. In addition to those that are attached to the endoplasmic reticulum, others move around the cytoplasm.

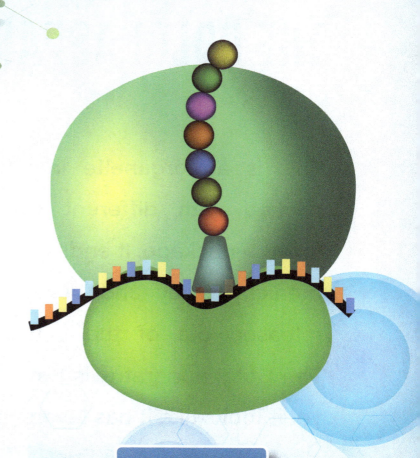

Ribosomes

THE GOLGI APPARATUS

This is an organelle in which different proteins get packed with different substances. The combination forms a package. It ends up breaking away and being released out of the cell. The Golgi apparatus is flat, yet it looks like it has layers stacked atop each other.

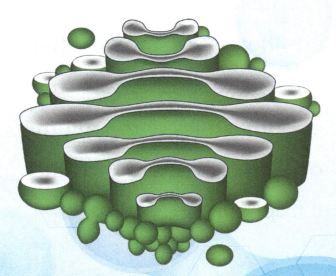

Golgi Apparatus

VACUOLES

Vacuoles are organelles like tiny tanks which store and get rid of waste.

Vacuole of an eukaryotic cell.

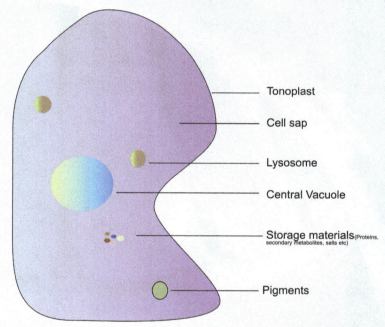

Tonoplast

Cell sap

Lysosome

Central Vacuole

Storage materials(Proteins, secondary metabolites, salts etc)

Pigments

Vacuole

Complex cells are known as eukaryotic cells. These cells have a nucleus and several organelles. They are found in both plants and animals. These types of cells are larger than the prokaryotic cells that are found in unicellular organisms. Prokaryotic cells are roughly ten times smaller than eukaryotic cells. Eukaryotic cells need to be bigger to hold all the different parts.

CELL MEMBRANE

LYSOSOME

MITOCHONDRION

GOLGI APPARATUS

RIBOSOMES

NUCLEOLUS

PEROXISOME

VACUOLE

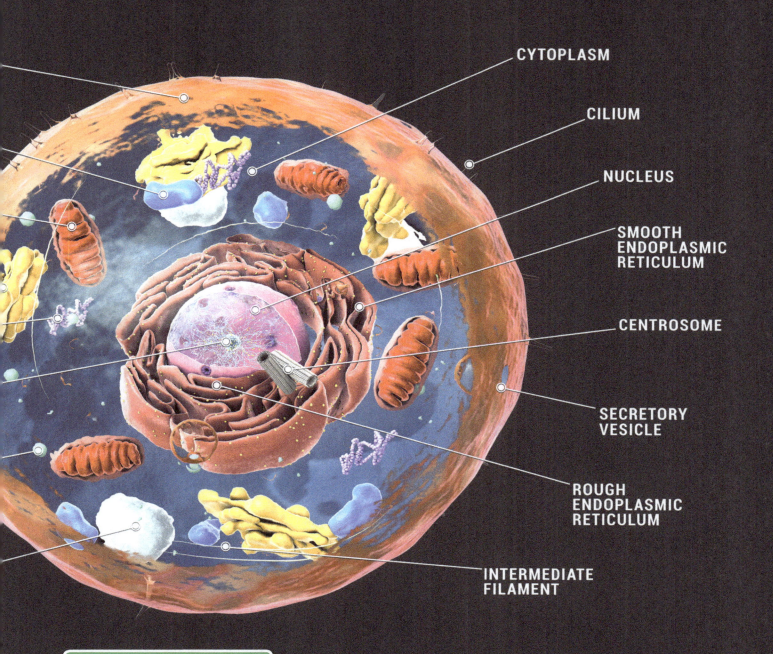

CYTOPLASM

CILIUM

NUCLEUS

SMOOTH
ENDOPLASMIC
RETICULUM

CENTROSOME

SECRETORY
VESICLE

ROUGH
ENDOPLASMIC
RETICULUM

INTERMEDIATE
FILAMENT

Labeled Eukaryotic cell.

45

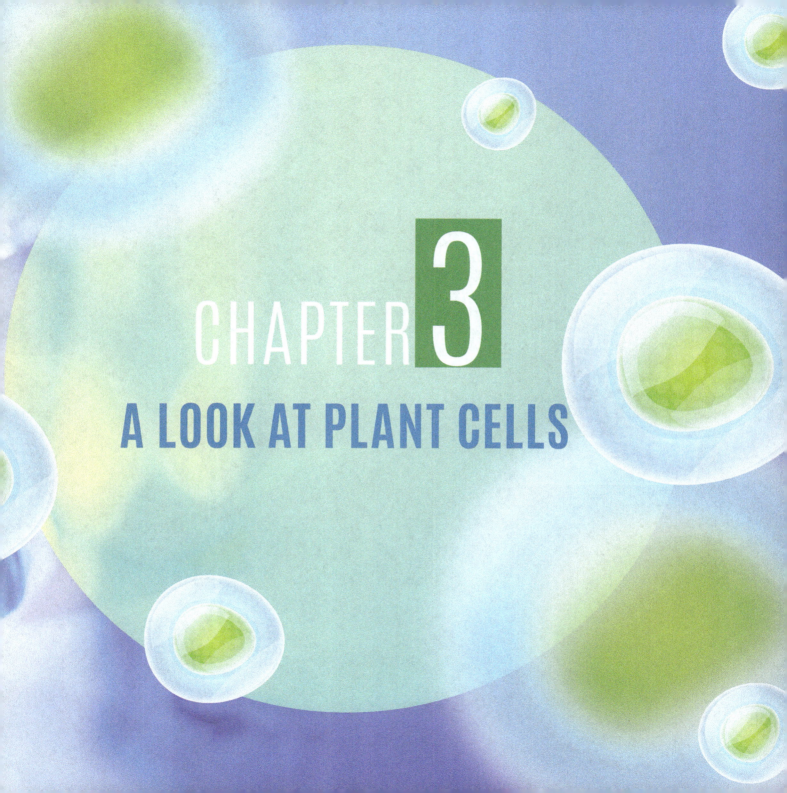

CHAPTER 3
A LOOK AT PLANT CELLS

Plants can be put into two categories. One category is vascular. The other is nonvascular.

Young plant growing.

VASCULAR PLANTS

Vascular plants rise higher from the surface of the ground than nonvascular plants do. Examples of vascular plants include trees, bushes, and flowers. They have stems, leaves, and roots.

Vascular plants have stems, leaves and roots.

They are equipped with tubes through which water and food are transported. These tubes are called xylem and phloem.

Diagram showing vascular tissue system in plants

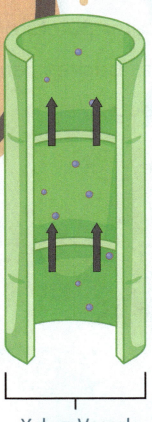

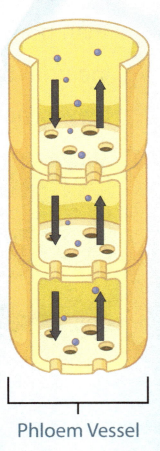

Xylem Vessel

Phloem Vessel

There are some differences among vascular plants. Their size, color, and shape may vary. Some are flowering plants while others are not. Examples of flowering plants are apple trees and roses. Examples of non-flowering plants are ferns and pine trees.

Apple Tree

Roses

Ferns

Pine Trees

NONVASCULAR PLANTS

Nonvascular plants are small and less complex than vascular plants. They lack leaves, stems, seeds, flowers, and roots. Also, they are not equipped with tubes through which food and water can be transported. They remain quite close to the surface of the ground. Examples include liverworts and moss.

Liverworts

Moss

Nonvascular plants inhabit moist areas. This is so that they can be near a source of water. Both vascular and nonvascular plants take in carbon dioxide. They make oxygen from it.

Nonvascular plants thrive in moist areas.

PARTS OF PLANT CELLS

There are parts of plant cells that are the same as those found in animal cells. They include the cell membrane, the nucleus, the mitochondria, the Golgi Apparatus, the Endoplasmic Reticulum, and ribosomes. Like with the animal cells, they will serve the same function or do the same job.

vacuole ———

chloroplast ———
cytoplasm ———
mitochondrion ———

cell membrane ———

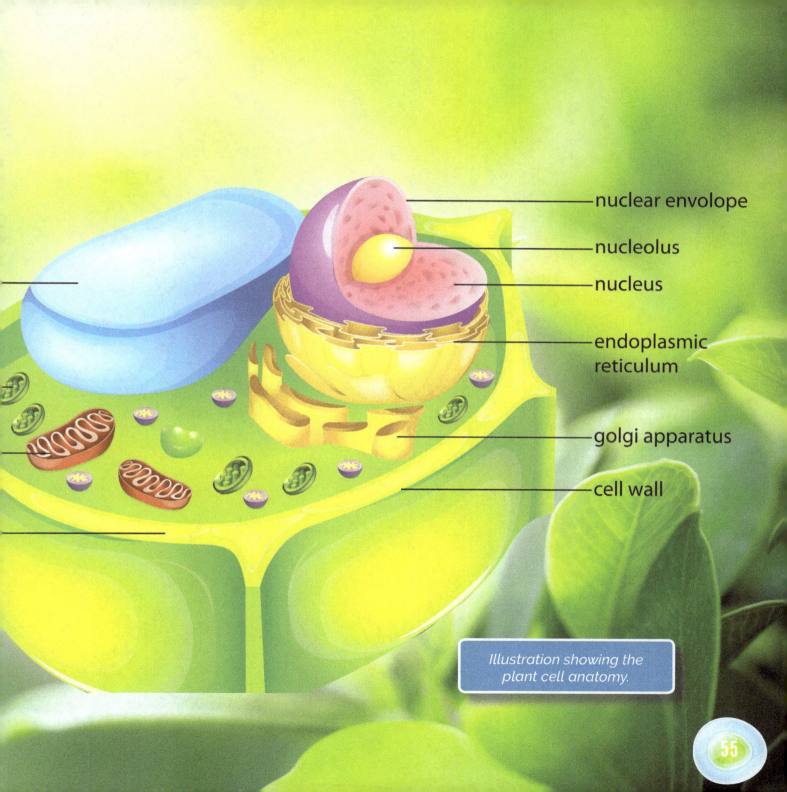

nuclear envolope

nucleolus

nucleus

endoplasmic reticulum

golgi apparatus

cell wall

Illustration showing the plant cell anatomy.

55

PARTS OF PLANT CELLS THAT ARE NOT IN ANIMALS

There are some parts of plant cells that are not found in the cells of animals. This section will look at these parts.

Plant cell under a microscope.

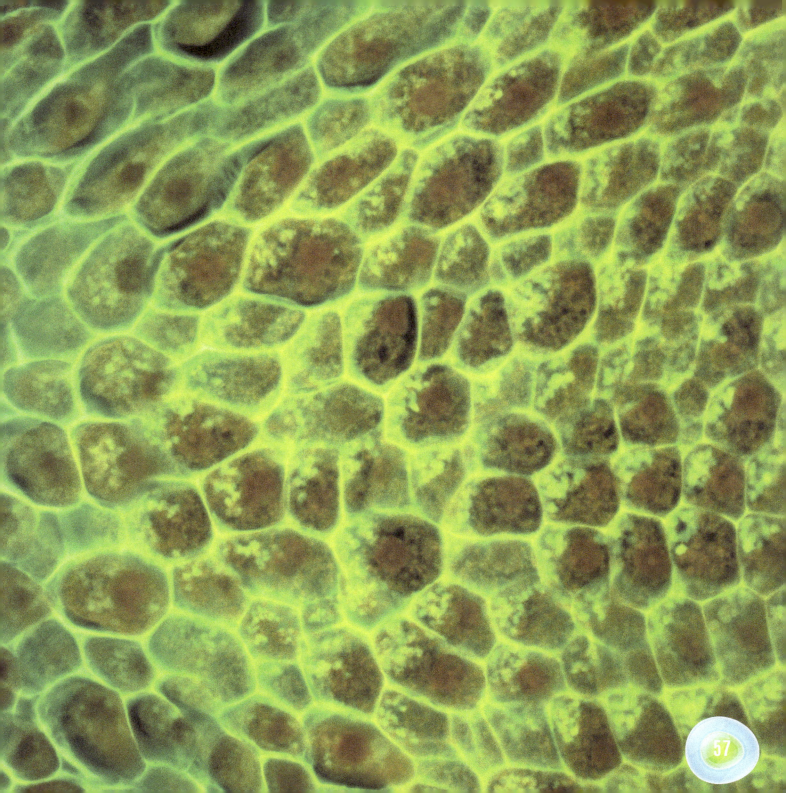

CELL WALL

The cell wall is not made up of living material. It consists of cellulose. This is a woody material or structure. Unlike animals, plants do not have anything to protect them against external elements. For this reason, the cell wall must be firm and rigid. By surrounding the cell membrane, it offers protection to it and the entire cell. It is a barrier to the outside. In addition, plants that grow tall need cellulose. It makes the plant stiff.

A diagram with plant cell walls structure and fiber scheme.

PLANT CELLULOSE

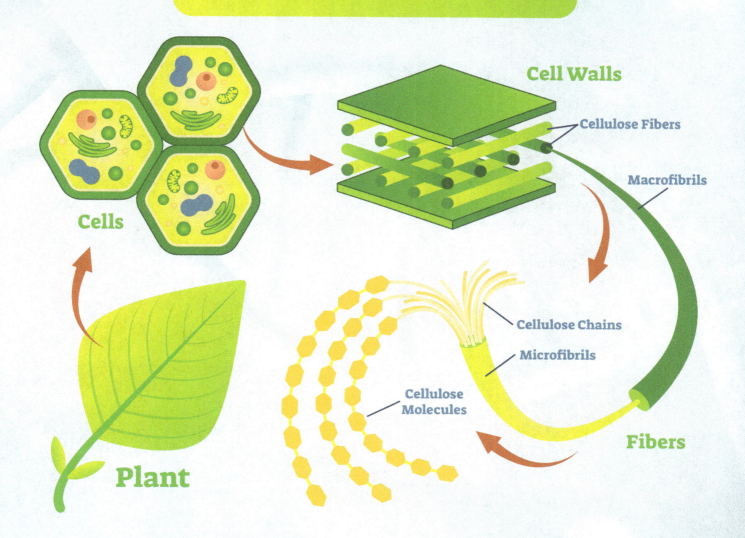

Cells

Plant

Cell Walls

Cellulose Fibers

Macrofibrils

Cellulose Chains

Microfibrils

Cellulose Molecules

Fibers

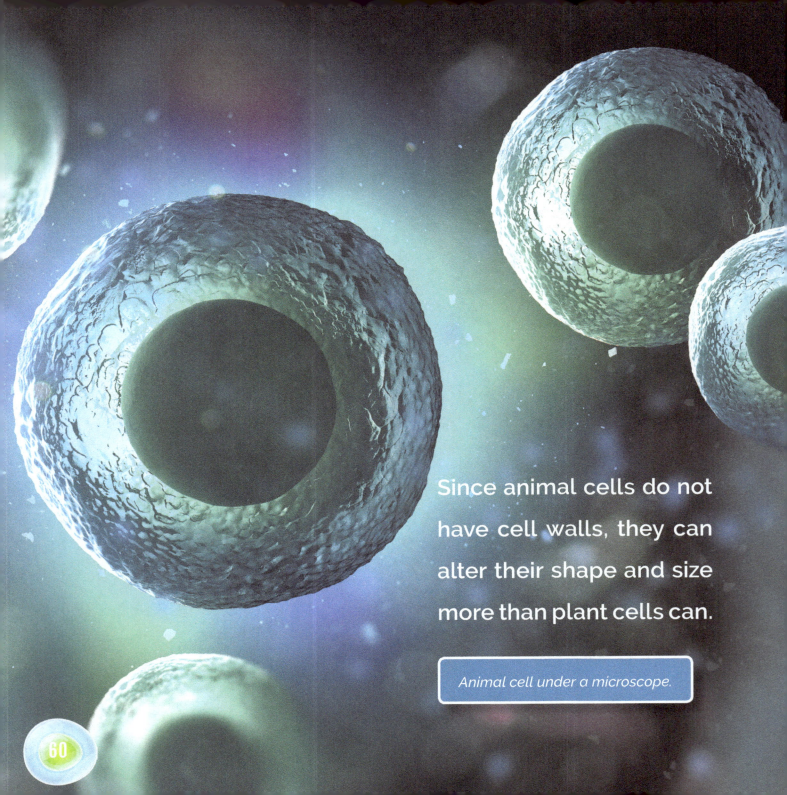

Since animal cells do not have cell walls, they can alter their shape and size more than plant cells can.

Animal cell under a microscope.

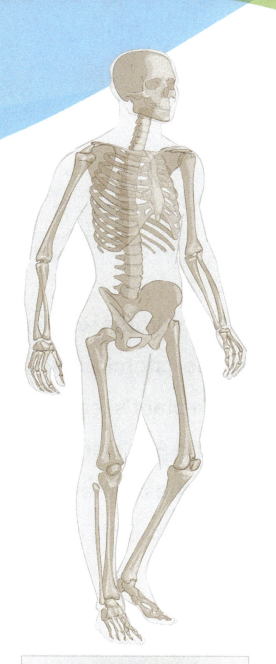

SKELETAL SYSTEM

Nonetheless, animals have other cells which function to build structures to support their bodies. Examples are bones which make up the skeletal system in humans.

A human skeletal system.

CHLOROPLASTS

There are certain plants which have chloroplasts. They hold the plant's chlorophyll. This is the chemical which makes a plant green. It can be found in a plant's leaves, for example. It is responsible for trapping the Sun's energy as it shines on the plant. Through photosynthesis, the energy converts carbon dioxide and water into food. This is how a plant gets its nutrition.

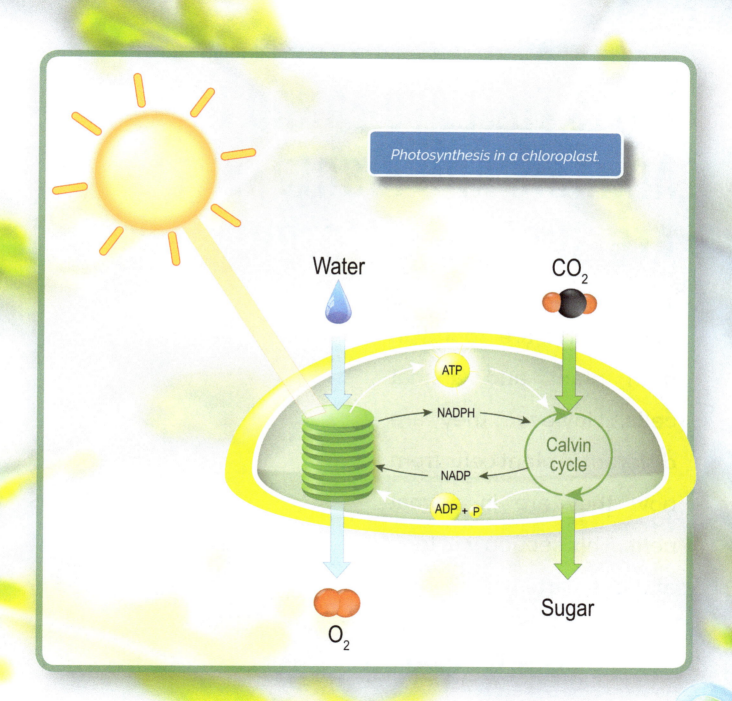

Photosynthesis in a chloroplast.

Water

CO_2

ATP

NADPH

Calvin cycle

NADP

ADP + P

O_2

Sugar

Parts That Are Found In Both Animals And Plants, But Are Slightly Different

Some parts are found in both plant and animal cells. However, they are different in plant cells from how they are in animal cells. This section will look at these parts.

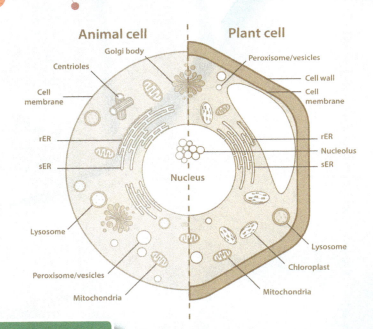

Animal cell
- Golgi body
- Centrioles
- Cell membrane
- rER
- sER
- Lysosome
- Peroxisome/vesicles
- Mitochondria

Plant cell
- Peroxisome/vesicles
- Cell wall
- Cell membrane
- rER
- Nucleolus
- sER
- Lysosome
- Chloroplast
- Mitochondria

Nucleus

Comparison between plant and animal cells.

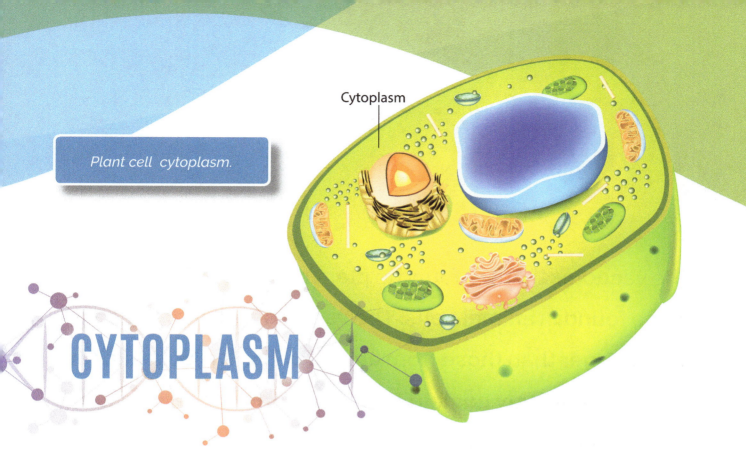

Cytoplasm

CYTOPLASM

Like an animal cell, a plant cell has cytoplasm. However, the plant's cytoplasm has special protein as well as certain compounds that provide shape for the plant. This is because a plant does not have a skeletal system like an animal does.

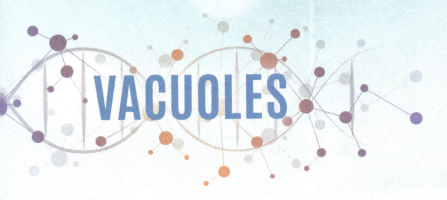

VACUOLES

The vacuoles that are found in plant cells are different than those found in animal cells. The vacuoles of plant cells are much larger than those from animal cells. It is possible for a plant cell to only contain one vacuole. However, it will be so big that it will force the other organelles of the cell off to the sides.

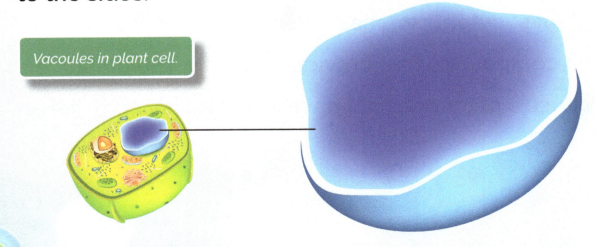

Vacoules in plant cell.

PARTS OF ANIMAL CELLS THAT ARE NOT IN PLANTS

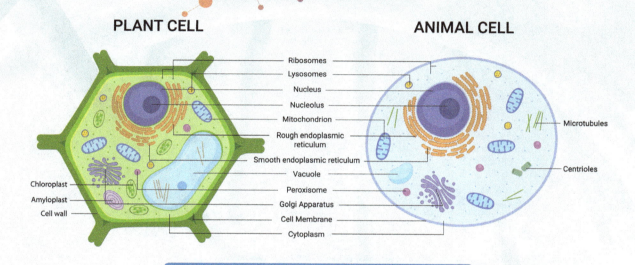

PLANT CELL   ANIMAL CELL

Ribosomes
Lysosomes
Nucleus
Nucleolus
Mitochondrion
Rough endoplasmic reticulum
Smooth endoplasmic reticulum
Vacuole
Peroxisome
Golgi Apparatus
Cell Membrane
Cytoplasm

Chloroplast
Amyloplast
Cell wall

Microtubules

Centrioles

Plant and Animal cell anatomy structure.

Some parts are not found in plant cells, but they are found in animal cells. Neither centrosomes nor lysosomes are contained in plant cells. Both are in animal cells.

Robert Hooke

DID YOU KNOW?

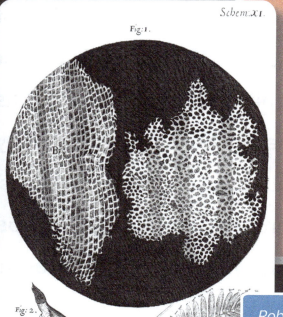

The person who came up with the name cell for the basic building blocks of an organism was Robert Hooke. He was a scientist from England. One day he was observing a tiny piece of cork under a microscope. The cork's different parts made him think of tiny rooms found in jails. For this reason, he decided to call them cells.

Robert Hooke's handwritten notes on cork cells

All organisms have cells. An organism is something which is alive. A cell is the smallest unit which makes up any kind of organism. Some have more cells than others. A unicellular organism only has one cell. A multicellular organism has many cells. Plants and animals are both living things. They have many cells. Some of their cells contain the same parts. Some parts can only be found in animals. Some can only be found in plants. There are other parts which are found in both, but have slightly different characteristics.